The Camp Survival Handbook

THE
CAMP SURVIVAL
H·A·N·D·B·O·O·K

by Katy Hall and Lisa Eisenberg
illustrated by David Neuhaus

HarperFestival®

A Division of HarperCollins*Publishers*

Contents

Are You Ready for Camp?

So you're thinking about going away to camp this summer? (If you're *not*, why in the world are you reading this book? Why don't you put it down and pick up some other light summer reading, like *The Joy of Folding Laundry* or *Lawn-Mowing for Fun and Profit*?)

Before you decide whether you are 100% ready to leave home for a couple of weeks—or maybe even a couple of months—the first all-important question you need to ask yourself is:

"Am I *really really really* ready to go to camp this summer?"

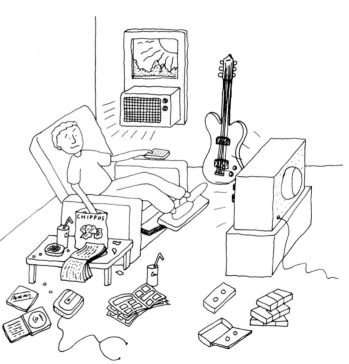

To find out, sharpen that old #2 pencil you haven't picked up since school let out and put an X next to each answer that really and truly describes *you*.

1. *Since school has been out, I have used the phrase "I'm bored" the following number of times:*

a. ___ 9 times.

b. ___ 93 times.

c. ___ 930 times.

d. ___ 9,300 times—and school only let out an hour ago!

2. *In the last week, my most exciting activity has been:*

a. ___ Staging pretend wrestling matches between my sister's old Surfer Barbie and my pet hamster, Gorgo.

b. ___ Flossing.

c. ___ Organizing my sock drawer by pattern, color, and number of holes.

d. ___ Seeing what happens when I mix Kool-Aid, barbecue sauce, toothpaste, shampoo, and leftover chicken salad.

3. *Lately the shows I've been watching on TV are:*

a. ___ Game shows made in 1972.

b. ___ Floor-wax commercials.

c. ___ *Star Trek* reruns that I've already seen 30 times.

d. ___ All of the above—and that's just my morning schedule!

4. *Yesterday I read:*

a. ___ The back of each and every cereal box in the cupboard.

b. ___ The license plate of each and every car that passed our house.

c. ___ My palm.

d. ___ Now that you mention it, in the days since school let out, I've forgotten how to read. In fact, someone's reading this book to me right now!

5. *So far this summer I've been getting up:*

a. ___ at 5:30 A.M. to do all the house and yardwork, then make breakfast in bed for the whole family.

b. ___ at noon.

c. ___ in time to catch three hours of back-to-back soap operas.

d. ___ Who gets up?

6. *This summer I've been exercising by:*

a. ___ Seeing how many times an hour I can yawn.

b. ___ Opening bags of corn chips.

c. ___ Arm wrestling with my pet hamster, Gorgo.

d. ___ Exercising? You're kidding, right?

If you put an X next to *any single answer on this test,* you're more than ready to go away to camp—in fact, the sooner you go, the better! And what about you would-be campers who *didn't* put an X next to even one answer on the test?

Don't worry! All that means is that you've forgotten how to make an X, you never knew how to make an X, you were sleeping when the test was given, or you've been getting so little exercise that you no longer had the strength to pick up the pen, pencil, or crayon you needed to take the test. Hey, don't worry about it! All these little problems can be solved easily. Where, you ask? Where *else*? Wake up and smell the powdered scrambled eggs!

AT SUMMER CAMP! (For Pete's sake, look at the title of this book!)

You: Before Camp

This diagram shows what you probably look like now, at this very moment, *before* your summer gets into full swing. Before you've read this valuable guidebook. Before you've been to camp.

Study the diagram. Then go to the mirror and take a good look. (Take a *long* look. If you're leaving for camp soon, it may be the last mirror you'll see all

Functional brain

New baseball cap

Recently-styled hair

Cool earrings

Study bags under eyes

Add-a-pearl necklace from Aunt Susie

Eager smile

"Save the Planet" T-shirt

Clean neck

This book

Trendy shorts

Brand-new white sneakers

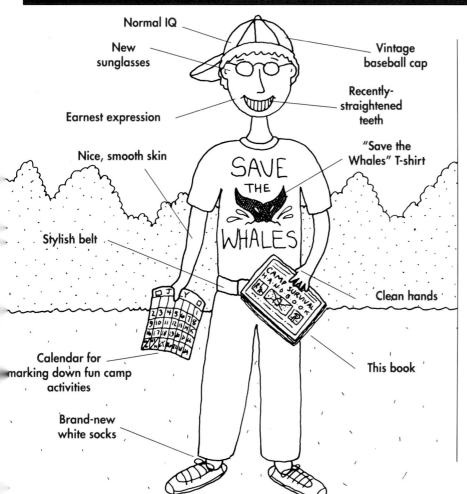

Normal IQ

New sunglasses

Vintage baseball cap

Recently-straightened teeth

Earnest expression

Nice, smooth skin

"Save the Whales" T-shirt

SAVE THE WHALES

Stylish belt

Clean hands

Calendar for marking down fun camp activities

This book

Brand-new white socks

summer!) Say good-bye to yourself—the old pre-camp, well-clothed, well-washed, well-adjusted (well, okay, maybe not *that* well-adjusted, or you wouldn't be reading this book!), well-fed YOU. Because, trust us, camp is going to change you big time. *If*, that is, you survive it at all. And that's where *we* come in. . . .

Next time you look in the mirror—if they have such a thing where you're going—you may see a change or two. So be prepared!

Is Camp Ready for You?

Hold it. You may be ready for camp, but is the camp you have chosen ready to roll out the red carpet and receive *you*? More important, is this camp worthy of having Y-O-U as one of its campers?

Has the tennis instructor, for example, made it to the finals at Wimbledon at least once? Does its arts 'n' crafts cabin have the tools to let you express yourself with, say, body tattooing?

Now is the time to decide:

Is Camp Ready for You?

Put an X on the line before the phrase that most accurately describes your chosen camp—or at least what it says your camp is like in that expensive, glossy brochure.

1. *The bus that will take you to camp has:*
a. ___ Air-conditioning.
b. ___ A color TV and a VCR.
c. ___ Reclining seats.
d. ___ None of the above.

2. *The counselor who meets your bus when you arrive at camp has:*
a. ___ Someone waiting nearby to carry your duffel bag.
b. ___ Someone waiting nearby to carry your comic book collection.
c. ___ Someone waiting nearby to carry you.
d. ___ None of the above.

3. *Your cabin has:*

a. ___ Maid service.

b. ___ Room service.

c. ___ A fully-stocked refrigerator.

d. ___ None of the above.

4. *The camp dining hall serves:*

a. ___ 28 flavors of ice cream.

b. ___ Nothing but yummy junk food.

c. ___ Curly fries.

d. ___ None of the above.

5. *The swimming area has:*

a. ___ Crystal-clear water and white-sand beaches.

b. ___ A wave machine for surfing.

c. ___ A heater.

d. ___ None of the above.

6. *The camp wakes you up each morning by:*

a. ___ Serving you breakfast in bed.

b. ___ Having your robe and bunny slippers waiting.

c. ___ Wake you up? They wouldn't dare!

d. ___ None of the above.

7. *For breakfast, your camp is likely to serve:*

a. ___ Two fried eggs, over easy, with a side of bacon and crustless toast.

b. ___ A fresh bagel, lightly toasted, with cream cheese and homemade strawberry preserves.

c. ___ A chocolate doughnut and a vanilla milkshake.

d. ___ None of the above.

8. *At a cookout you are most likely to be grilling:*

a. ___ A nice, juicy steak, medium rare.

b. ___ A quarter pound of lean ground beef molded into a patty.

c. ___ A foot-long hot dog topped with down-home chili.

d. ___ None of the above.

You say you checked most of the **d** answers? Welcome to the real world, camper. Now that you've figured out that you're headed for *summer camp,* and not to one of the hot spots you've seen on *Lifestyles of the Rich and Famous,* here are the real **d** answers.

1. A nonworking toilet with a major odor problem.

2. Someone waiting nearby to watch you carry your 50-pound duffel bag for the six-mile hike to the camp.

3. Walls—if you're lucky.

4. Exactly what they serve down at your local bus station.

5. More than a dozen species of rare algae.

6. Setting off the air-raid siren it inherited from the military base that used to be where your camp is now.

7. Powdered eggs and Spam.

8. Dog food.

Whew! So now that *that's* settled, it's time to . . .

Start Packing!

Any camp worth its weight in nametags will have already sent you a list of the things you need to bring from home, such as a sleeping bag, a flashlight, a jackknife, and a rain poncho. But here's a checklist of all the *other* important items your camp might have forgotten to tell you about.

What to Bring to Camp

- ☐ insect repellent
- ☐ extra insect repellent
- ☐ Ticks-Off Moisture Pack
- ☐ fly swatter
- ☐ mosquito netting
- ☐ Raid
- ☐ Sting-away Bee Sting Balm
- ☐ a back scratcher
- ☐ Chiggers Begone! spray

- ☐ Gnats *Not!* (economy size)
- ☐ Calamine lotion
- ☐ Bactine
- ☐ cotton balls
- ☐ hospital gown

Now that you know what you should bring to camp, it's also important to know what you shouldn't bring to camp.

That's why we've developed the following checklist:

What NOT to Bring to Camp

- ☐ a three-week supply of mocha-almond ice cream pops
- ☐ your pet hamster, Gorgo
- ☐ the sweater your grandmother spent three years knitting for you
- ☐ your family's new CD player
- ☐ your best dress-up shoes
- ☐ the microwave
- ☐ your deluxe Nintendo home entertainment center
- ☐ your rubber ducky
- ☐ your sister's old Surfer Barbie
- ☐ your parents

Your Counselor

When you arrive at camp, one of the first people you'll meet will be your camp counselor, who, strangely enough, has a very good chance of being nicknamed either Pixie or Moose. (If your counselor's nickname is Hurly, Barfy, Spitsy, Coughy, Burpy, Urpy, or Doc, you've caught the bus to Camp Uppsie-Whoopsie. Call home and get picked up *immediately*!)

Ideally, Pixie and Moose will look something like these guys.

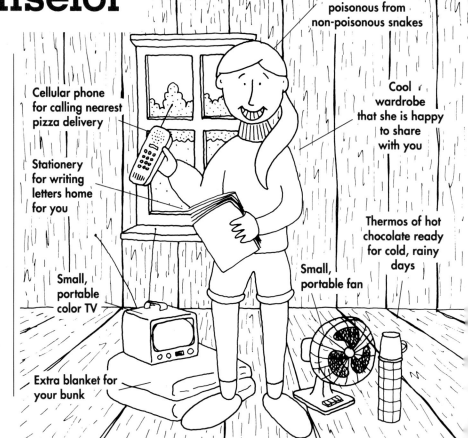

Cellular phone for calling nearest pizza delivery

Stationery for writing letters home for you

Small, portable color TV

Extra blanket for your bunk

Knows how to tell poisonous from non-poisonous snakes

Cool wardrobe that she is happy to share with you

Thermos of hot chocolate ready for cold, rainy days

Small, portable fan

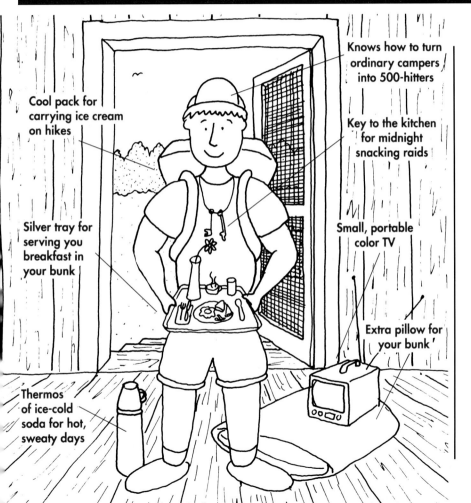

Knows how to turn ordinary campers into 500-hitters

Cool pack for carrying ice cream on hikes

Key to the kitchen for midnight snacking raids

Silver tray for serving you breakfast in your bunk

Small, portable color TV

Extra pillow for your bunk

Thermos of ice-cold soda for hot, sweaty days

We can't repeat too often that having a good relationship with Pixie or Moose will be very important to your survival at summer camp. We can't repeat too often that having a good relationship with Pixie or Moose will be very important to your survival at summer camp.

Here are some things your counselor will undoubtedly say when you first meet him or her. Put an X next to the response you think is most likely to make Moose or Pixie adore you right off the bat.

Moose/Pixie: Howdy, camper! Welcome to Camp Mini-Ha-Ha-Ha!

You:

___ **1)** Where's the bathroom? I feel sick!

___ **2)** Howdy! Here's a ten-pound tin of homemade chocolate-chip cookies. And there's plenty more where this came from!

Moose/Pixie: Let's you and me tote those bags of yours to the bunkhouse.

You:

___ **1)** What? You mean I'm expected to carry my own luggage?

___ **2)** Oh, please, I'd like to carry everything by myself. That way, maybe by the end of the summer I'll be in the same terrific shape you are!

Moose/Pixie: Wait'll you meet the other campers you'll be bunking with. They're a great bunch. You're going to love them.

You:

___ **1)** Right. And I'm Yogi Bear.

___ **2)** Would you be interested in a live-in servant to help out in the counselors' air-conditioned bunkhouse? I have great references!

Moose/Pixie: What made you decide to come to Camp Mini-Ha-Ha-Ha?

You:

___ **1)** My parents. It was the cheapest camp they could find.

___ **2)** I begged to come here after I saw the picture of *you* in the camp brochure!

Moose/Pixie: We'll all head down to the lodge for dinner when Cookie hits the gong. The chow's terrific here!

You:

___ **1)** Where's the bathroom? I feel sick!

___ **2)** Before I left home, I sewed a month-long supply of junk food into the lining of my sleeping bag. If you'll let me skip dinner, I'll split it with you.

Clearly, those of you who put your X next to the number **2** answers are destined to be happy campers. And what about those of you who chose the number **1** answers? Well, let's just say it looks as if you'll probably be spending a lot of time in the bathroom this summer . . . *hiding from your counselor*!

Surviving Nicknames

You've arrived at camp with the right stuff, and you've made Pixie or Moose your pal for the rest of the summer. So on to the next important moves you need to make in order to survive the summer—and possibly even have a good time.

In almost every camp in the nation (and even some camps in Freedonia), you'll be slapped with a nickname the instant you trudge through those rustic pine-

log gates. Usually the first nickname you're called is the one that sticks with you for the rest of the summer . . . just like a dead fly on a wet lollipop.

So what's in a name, you say? You wouldn't mind being known as "Slim" or "Lefty" for a month or two? Of course not! But think, for a minute, about the *other* possibilities. What if you make the mistake of showing up at camp with your favorite souvenir Donald Duck cap perched on top of your head? Do you *really* want to spend the entire summer being known as "Quack Brain"? Or maybe "Beak Head"? No way!

All you have to do to survive the nickname ordeal is study our Nickname Dos and Don'ts. It's the only way to be sure of getting the *right* name for yourself.

Nickname Dos and Don'ts

DO pass out red-hot cinnamon candy the instant you get to camp. If you're lucky, this will earn you a great nickname like "Fireball" or maybe even "Hot Stuff."

DON'T bring your ant farm to camp—no matter how attached you are to those little critters. It can only lead to nicknames like "Bug," "Six Legs," or, worse yet, maybe even "Larva." (Unfortunately, because it's the only kind of wildlife they've ever seen, all the city kids will definitely call you "Cockroach.")

DO tell everyone you're from out west—no matter where you're really from. "Tex," "Nevada," "Colorado," "Dakota," and "Montana" are all totally cool nicknames.

DON'T tell anyone you're from New Jersey. Being called "Newark," "Trenton," "New Brunswick," or "Montclair" is totally uncool.

DO choose your snack foods carefully. "Banana Lips," "Dorito Breath," and "The Jolly Rancher" are all frightening possibilities.

DO arrive at camp carrying either a surfboard or a skateboard. The other campers will immediately start calling you "Surfer Dude" or "Skater Dude" or maybe even just "Dude"—all highly desirable nicknames.

If anyone does try to stick you with an uncool nickname, **DO** fight back! Say "If you tell anyone my nickname is _____, I'll tell everyone that *your* nickname is:

(Pick one . . . pick two . . . hey, it's gonna be a long summer, pick 'em all!)

❏ Weasel Face   ❏ Fishlips

❏ Fungus   ❏ Toe Jam

- ❏ Vermin
- ❏ Bump
- ❏ Maggot
- ❏ Slime Nose
- ❏ Grub
- ❏ Chigger
- ❏ Rodent
- ❏ Earwax

- ❏ Tinkerbell
- ❏ Gleech
- ❏ Jellyfish
- ❏ Worm Brain
- ❏ Dog Breath
- ❏ Igor
- ❏ Burp
- ❏ Dingbat

Hey, FUNGUS!

Just remember, everyone's in the same boat at camp—and that's the *name* of the game!

Surviving the Old Campers

If this is your first summer at your chosen camp, you are a *new camper*. (No duh!) And even in the seventh week of camp, you'll still be a *new camper* to those snotty kids who have been to the camp before. It's an unfortunate fact of camp life that, unless this is the very first year of business for the camp you are attending (in which case, good luck, guinea pigs!), there will always be those know-it-all kids who've been to the camp before.

These "old campers" may not be old at all. In fact, they may be younger than you are, which makes them even more obnoxious for trying to tell you exactly how everything is done at camp and trying to scare you with their horror stories of "last summer."

Your insect repellent won't work against these pesky old campers. In this combat your best weapon is your tongue. No, we don't mean you should make faces at the old campers. And for sure you shouldn't lick them. Yuk! Just use your tongue to say these wild and witty comebacks.

Old Camper: Oh, you're in chipmunk bunk? Last summer everyone in that bunk got bitten by mosquitoes that carried sleeping sickness.

You: Big deal. At the camp I went to last summer we were all bitten by a werewolf.

You should see what happens to me when there's a full moon.

Old Camper: *He's* your counselor? Oh, no! He's the one everybody calls Swatter. Last year, when one kid didn't get up on time, Swatter tried to whack him with a fly swatter.

You: Like I'm *really* scared! At the camp I went to last summer my counselor was called Pit Bull. If you didn't get up the second the gong sounded, he'd take a bite out of your leg. Wanna see my scars?

Old Camper: You ever swum in a lake where there are leeches before?

You: Not really. The camp I went to last summer was on the ocean and there were sharks and sea serpents. It was scary at first, but I got used to it, and, boy, did it ever improve my time for the one-hundred-yard freestyle.

Old Camper: Hey, you talk like you think you're pretty tough. So tell me, what did they call you at that camp you went to last summer?

You: Your Highness.

Surviving Camp Food

TODAY'S LUNCH
Lake Fish
Gopher Surprise
Buzzard Burrito
Squid Salad
dogs
soup
jello

Pee-yew! What's that odor? Is it a skunk? An overturned garbage can? An overflowing outhouse? Nope. What you're smelling is . . . lunch.

Now, while your first reaction might be, "Where's the bathroom, I feel sick!" here are two simple words that will help you survive camp food. They are: BE CREATIVE!

If you can't stand to *eat* the food, why not put it to good use some other way? The ideas below may give you some food for thought—if not for your stomach!

The most important thing to remember about your meals at camp is this: Few of them are really as dangerous as they look.

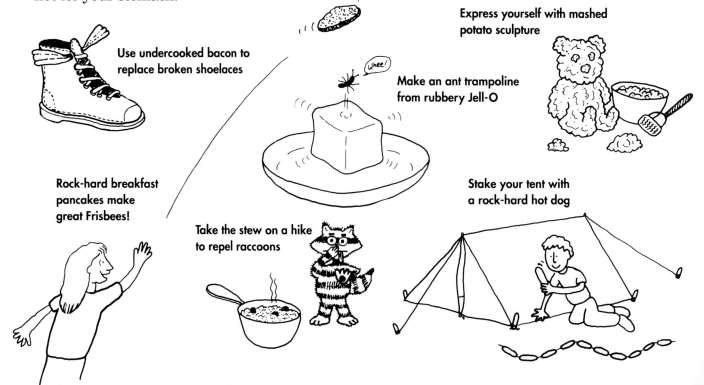

Use undercooked bacon to replace broken shoelaces

Express yourself with mashed potato sculpture

Whee!

Make an ant trampoline from rubbery Jell-O

Rock-hard breakfast pancakes make great Frisbees!

Take the stew on a hike to repel raccoons

Stake your tent with a rock-hard hot dog

To help you survive camp food—you guessed it!—we have put together a list of Top Ten Table Tips.

Recite this pledge before every meal.

This Summer, Here at Camp, I Promise Never, Ever to . . .

1. Eat anything while it is still moving.

2. Eat anything that has "surprise" as part of its name.

3. Be the first to taste any dish at my table.

4. Eat anything that the camp dog has passed up.

5. Eat anything that made my camp counselor pass out.

6. Be talked into trading my dessert for my bunkmate's meat loaf.

7. Ask, "What is it?"

8. Eat anything that has "mystery" as part of its name.

9. Eat anything that I carved my initials in at a previous meal.

10. Ask for seconds.

Surviving Ants

What kind of ants are you likely to meet at camp? Gi-*ants*! And you'd better *bee* prepared! This diagram shows you the main parts of the typical camp ant you'll be running into—and away from—this summer.

Your Pet Hamster, Gorgo (for size comparison)

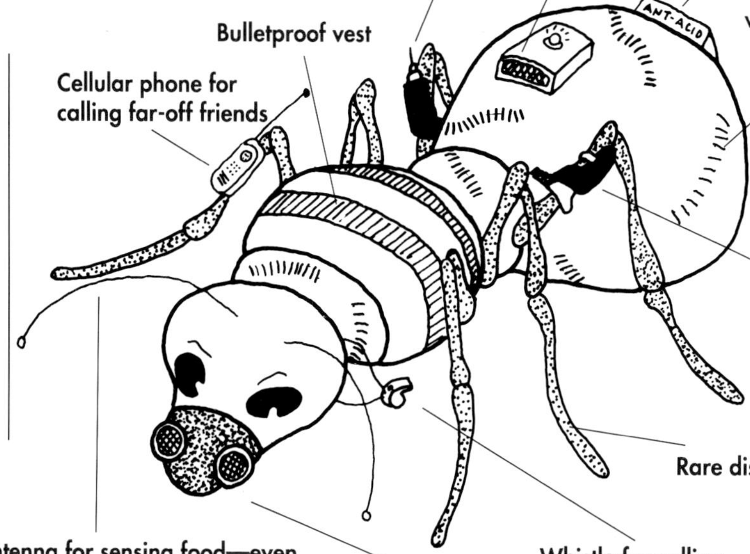

Radar detector

Ant-acid tablet

High-powered drill

Scars from battles with King Kong and Godzilla

Bulletproof vest

Cellular phone for calling far-off friends

Laser stun gun

Rare disease germs

Antenna for sensing food—even when it's stuck in your braces

Gas mask

Whistle for calling nearby friends

The Common Immature Ant
(shown smaller than actual size—you should see the <u>mature</u> one!)

Surviving the Camp Infirmary

You say your throat feels a little scratchy? Your poison ivy is spreading? Join the club! This diagram shows the condition of the typical camper after just two days of camp life. If you have any (or all) of these symptoms, you're probably thinking it's time for a visit to the camp nurse.

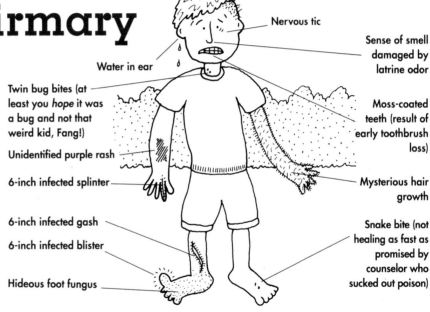

Mysterious hair loss

Fevered brain worried about that throbbing raccoon scratch

Nervous tic

Sense of smell damaged by latrine odor

Water in ear

Twin bug bites (at least you *hope* it was a bug and not that weird kid, Fang!)

Unidentified purple rash

6-inch infected splinter

6-inch infected gash

6-inch infected blister

Hideous foot fungus

Moss-coated teeth (result of early toothbrush loss)

Mysterious hair growth

Snake bite (not healing as fast as promised by counselor who sucked out poison)

Yes, if you look like this, you probably think you really really need to see the nurse. So turn the page, and . . .

THINK AGAIN!

STETHOSCOPE to stick in ears to block out sounds of patients' screaming

PHONE for dialing 1-800-I-LUV-CUT for advice on first-time procedures

COIL OF ROPE for rodeo day or reluctant patients

HUGE HYPO for minor sore throats, insect bites, sunburn

GET ME OUT OF HERE PLEASE PLEASE PLEASE

OPERATING TABLE for minor sore throats, insect bites, sunburn

DOG (surgical assistant)

HUGE CARVING KNIFE for minor sore throats, insect bites, sunburn, amputations, arguments with whining campers

BOX OF TISSUES for minor cuts, major cuts, hemorrhages, gunshot wounds

Surviving the Swim Test

What happened to the camper who fell into the lake right before the swim test? She got wet!

The diagrams on this page show the strokes you will be required to perform to pass your camp swim test.

The front crawl

The backstroke

The butterfly

The breaststroke

So what if you can't do any of these strokes? No problem! All you have to do to be in the swim of things is bring one simple piece of equipment from home!

Surviving on the Tennis Court

If you're attending the fancy, high-priced camp you picked out, you'll be receiving professional-quality, one-on-one tennis instruction on a well-tended, air-conditioned, indoor court. On the other hand, if you're attending Camp-o El Cheap-o your *parents* picked out, you'll be part of a thirty-person group tennis lesson on a court that could double as a miniature golf course, complete with water hazards and scampering wildlife.

If that's the case, you'll need the following handy tips:

What to Do with Your Tennis Racquet While You're Waiting for Your Lesson to Start:

1. Slay your enemies.

2. Scratch those hard-to-reach places.

3. Rock out.

4. Settle disputes.

5. Batter up!

Surviving Arts 'n' Crafts

Just because you'd never heard of a lanyard before you came to camp doesn't mean you don't want to make one. Go ahead, pick out your colors of plastic string.

You say you want to skip the hideous lanyard keychains and go right for the big time? Make something you might actually *use* once you get home? Then have a look at our list of fabulous things you can create with materials available at the Arts 'n' Crafts Center.

Arts n' Crafts
Key chains
ashtrays
lanyards
rocket launcher

Project 1: Collar for your dog

Materials needed: 2 12-inch pieces of plastic string in different colors; 1 small silver buckle; spikes (optional)

Comments: Since your dog would turn up his sensitive canine nose at any doggie bag you'd bring him from the dining hall, why not bring him a collar that will add a little color to his life?

Project 2: Collar for your pet hamster, Gorgo

Materials needed: 2 6-inch pieces of plastic string in different colors; 1 small silver buckle; spikes (optional)

Comments: Since Gorgo isn't too big, this project won't take long.

Project 3: Belt for your sister's old Surfer Barbie

Materials needed: 2 3-inch pieces of plastic string in different colors; 1 teensy-weensy silver buckle; spikes (optional)

Comments: Barbie's waist is probably just a little wider than your thumb, so this is a really short-term project.

WARNING: Should you attempt both projects 2 and 3, be careful not to mix up Surfer Barbie's belt with Gorgo's collar. (We are not responsible for the results!)

Project 4: Collar for your little brother or sister

Materials needed: 4 18-inch pieces of plastic string in different colors; one silver buckle; spikes (optional)

Comments: Don't tell the arts 'n' crafts counselor about this one! Your mom, either!

Project 5: Raccoon coat for mom or dad

Materials needed: 25 to 30 raccoons; bowie knife; hide scraper; skin stretcher; needle, thread, and thimble; buttons; monogram (optional)

Comments: Get an early start on this project, as it requires quite a bit of planning and hard work.

Surviving the Campfire

Songs to Sing Around the Campfire

"If You're Happy and You Know It"

"Found a Peanut"

"I've Been Workin' on the Railroad"

"Row, Row, Row Your Boat"

"Make New Friends"

"The More We Get Together"

"Frère Jacques"

"Oh, Susanna"

"The Happy Wanderer"

"Camptown Races"

"Kumbaya"

"He's Got the Whole World in His Hands"

"Come, Little Chipmunk, Warm Your Tail by Our Fire"

Songs NOT to Sing Around the Campfire

Theme from *America's Most Wanted*

Theme from *Nightmare on Elm Street*

"Strangers in the Night"

Anything from *The Stephen King Sing-Along Songbook*

Theme from *Jaws*

Theme from *Rescue 911*

Theme from *Unsolved Mysteries*

"If You're Homesick and You Know It"

"Bail, Bail, Bail Your Boat"

"Come, Little Rabid Raccoon, Warm Your Foaming Jaws by Our Fire"

A Campfire Ghost Story

Wait for a few other people to tell some lame ghost stories, like the one about the vindow viper or the one about the Ivory soap ("It floats! It floats!" Puh-*lease*!). Then, when there's a lull in the conversation, say quietly:

"I know a story. It isn't really a ghost story. It's a true story. In fact, it happened to me at the camp I went to last summer. But [pause significantly here] . . . well, to be honest, maybe I shouldn't talk about it. It's just *too* frightening."

At this point, everyone will start begging you to tell your "true" story. After a while, give in and say:

It was a dark and starless night—a night much like this one. My friends and I were sitting around a campfire. It was a campfire much like this one. We were roasting hot dogs and marshmallows when all at once, my friend Tony cried, "Where is Pat? What's happened to our counselor?" All of us gasped because only seconds before Pat had been sitting there beside us. But

now Pat had vanished. Of course, we all agreed that someone had to go look for Pat. But no one felt like going off alone into the dark woods. Finally Tony stood up and plunged into the forest in search of Pat.

The rest of us waited and waited for Tony to come back. After what seemed like forever, no one stepped out of the woods. At last, my friend Chris reluctantly agreed to go look for Tony.

The rest of us waited and waited for Chris to come back. But once again no one stepped out of the woods. Now only two of us were left.

After another long while I convinced Lee to go look for Chris. I waited and waited for Lee to come back. But once again no one stepped out of the woods. One by one, each and every camper had disappeared into the forest, and I was the only one left by the fire. Imagine my fear as I sat there, shivering and alone, wondering what in the world to do. And then the sounds began. A low, eerie moaning filled the air. Someone—or something—was approaching through the woods.

Step . . . step . . . step.

"Pat?" I called out. "Tony?"

An unearthly moan was my only answer.

"OOOOOOOH!"

Step . . . step . . . step.

My hair stood on end.

The steps were getting closer. And closer.

"Chris? Lee?" I called.

Oooooooooh!

Step . . . step . . . step. Suddenly a shadow fell over the fire. I turned and saw something step out of the woods, and I jumped and . . .

At this point in your story, jump up, put your hands around another camper's neck,

open your mouth, and cry out with your loudest, most bloodcurdling scream!

"EEEEEEIIIIAAAUUUUGGGHHHH!"

This may well be the finest moment of your entire summer. Without a doubt everyone will say you're the champion storyteller of all time—once they stop screaming, that is!

A word of caution: Choose your victim with care. You *probably* want to avoid selecting a camper with any of the following:

1. a heart condition

2. a violent temper

3. a large older brother

4. a weapon

Surviving Stargazing

One of your favorite nighttime activities at camp will definitely be stargazing. No, no, you won't be meeting Jason Priestley or Madonna. You'll be leaving your nice warm bunk, going out into the chilly, damp night, with ants and snakes slithering all around you, and you'll be asked to believe that the stars in the sky that look like this:

are actually constellations forming pictures like this:

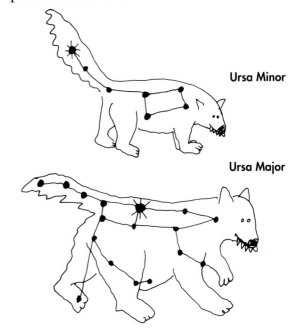

Ursa Minor

Ursa Major

But use your imagination and you can see *this* in the sky!

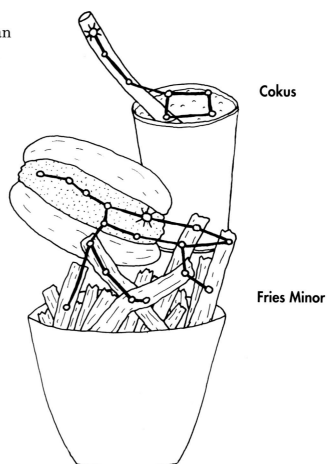

Cokus

Burger Major

Fries Minor

Surviving Camp Pranks

You say you twisted your ankle on the seven-mile nature hike? Your canoe tipped over? The new specimen you added to your leaf collection turned out to be poison ivy? Boy, are you ready for a good night's sleep. The cabin is mighty quiet as you crawl into your bed and . . . Whoa! What's this? Your feet have hit a dead end! Shove and push as you might, you just can't seem to get into your bed. As your bunkmates burst into giggles and a chorus of "Short-sheet! Short-sheet!" you realize you've been had! Or have you? You can have the last laugh yet—it all depends on how you react. Be cool!

But why wait until the pranks are pulled to see how cool you can be? Take our **Pranks Preview Test** right now!

1. *Your bunkmates short-sheet your bed. You:*

a. Cry until your sheet is sopping wet.

b. Call the parents of the campers involved and tell on them.

c. Short-sheet their beds tomorrow night!

d. Say, "Oh, what a cozy little bed!" Curl up and make obnoxious snoring sounds for half an hour or so.

2. *On a camp out someone puts a frog inside your sleeping bag. You:*

a. Scream hysterically.

b. Take the incident to Judge Wapner on *The People's Court*.

c. Put a frog in someone's sleeping bag tomorrow night!

d. Pretend to kiss the frog. Then run around and let Froggie give everyone else on the camp out a big good night kiss.

3. *In the dining hall, someone plants a plastic ant right in the middle of your mashed potatoes! You:*

a. Let out a bloodcurdling scream and faint.

b. March to the head table and tell the camp director exactly what happened.

c. Put a big plastic spider on someone else's mashed potatoes tomorrow night!

d. Say "Hello, Antie Em!" Wait until your counselor is looking the other way, scoop up a forkful of mashed potatoes with the ant on top, and fling the whole mess at the person sitting across from you.

Cool Analysis:

If you picked mostly **a** answers, you're a **screamer**. You're totally uncool—a prankpuller's dream. Prepare to be pranked all summer long!

If you picked mostly **b** answers you're a **tattletale**. You're the one prankpullers love to hate. Prepare to endure increasingly horrible pranks all summer long!

If you picked mostly **c** answers you're a **repeater**. Not too original maybe, but what the heck! It's campers like you who keep pranks going all summer long.

If you picked mostly **d** answers, you're an **ultracool camper**. Your responses are both fresh and original. Just be careful that they aren't *too* fresh and original or other creative prankpullers will be lying in wait to try new ones out on you all summer long.

Surviving Homesickness

When you first arrived at camp, everything was so new and exciting that you didn't have time to think about home. But now that you've settled into the routine of wake up, choke down food, hike, swim, choke down more food, hike, peel your sunburn, sing songs, burn hot dogs, sleep, you may wonder what's happening on the home front. You may even wish you were back home! As Dorothy said in *The Wizard of Oz*, "There's no place like home." Or is there? Remember . . .

1. How *you* have to scrape those repulsive plates every night after dinner while your little brother watches TV?

2. How *you* have to change the disgusting shavings in your pet hamster Gorgo's cage while your big sister yaps on the phone?

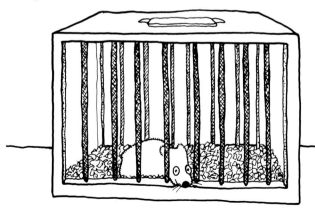

3. How *you* have to take out the stinky garbage while your little sister reads *your* comics?

4. How your big brother couldn't afford that weight-lifting equipment he wanted, so he decided to bench-press *you*?

5. How your mom has been nagging you to sit down and have that little talk about that three-year supply of unsigned report cards she found under your bed?

6. How your dad has been nagging you to sit down and have that BIG talk about the BIG phone bill that came after that four-hour call to your best friend who just moved to New Zealand?

7. How your cousin, Scarface, is spending the summer at your house so he can be closer to his parole officer?

8. How your cat, Chuck, has developed this little digestion problem that *you* always have to clean up?

9. How you promised your next-door neighbor that you'd help him clean out his septic tank in exchange for him keeping quiet about that ball you accidentally threw through his window?

And *now* do you remember how much you love to wake up, choke down food, hike, swim, choke down more food, hike, peel your sunburn, sing songs, burn hot dogs, and sleep?

We thought so.

Just Surviving

From the moment you wake up in the morning at camp, you'll be a-*mazed* at just how many activities you'll be desperate to avoid. Here's a maze to help you practice surviving an entire day without doing a single thing you don't want to do.

Your starting point? Curled in the fetal position in your nice, warm bunk. Your goal? The video arcade at the mall in town.

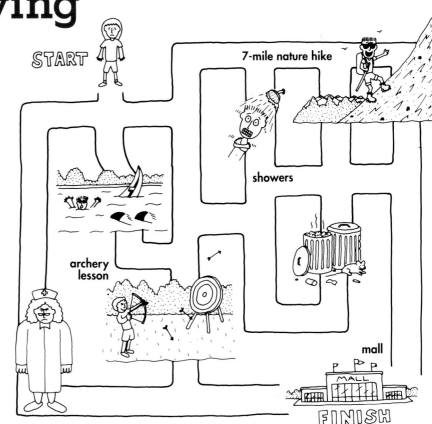

START

7-mile nature hike

showers

archery lesson

mall

MALL

FINISH

You: After Camp

You may be wondering if you've gotten your money's worth out of this little book. (Well, all right, you may have started wondering this a while back!) If you've followed all our advice, no doubt you'll wish you could send us a little extra money, because by now you are a well-seasoned, well-muscled, well-adjusted camper who's going to walk away with all the prizes on Awards Night.

Barely functional brain

Hair that's forgotten the meaning of the word "shampoo"

Peeling nose

Holes in ears where you once wore cool earrings

Raccoon-tooth necklace

Grimy crust on neck

Mysterious rash

Dirty "Save Me!" T-shirt

This book

Filthy trendy shorts

Dingy gray sneaker

43 hiking blisters on left foot alone

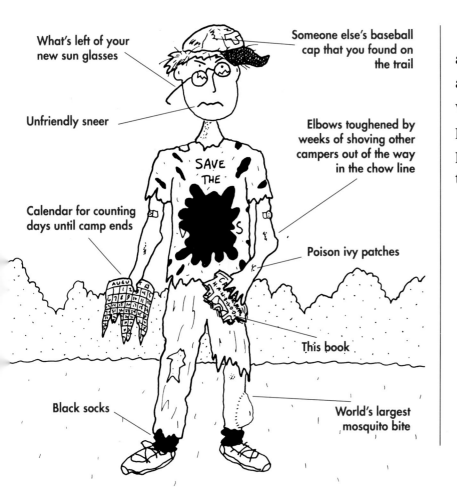

What's left of your new sun glasses

Someone else's baseball cap that you found on the trail

Unfriendly sneer

Elbows toughened by weeks of shoving other campers out of the way in the chow line

SAVE THE S

Calendar for counting days until camp ends

Poison ivy patches

This book

Black socks

World's largest mosquito bite

And if you *haven't* taken our advice to heart? If you've actually *ignored* our words of wisdom? *Tsk tsk*. Then you're probably a . . . Well, you probably look something like this.

Rate Your Camp

The weeks at camp have flown by and here it is, time to say good-bye to Pixie and Moose, time to play just one more prank.

So how was your camp? Would you recommend it to your friends? To your enemies? Here's a checklist to help you decide if your camp stacks up as well as those cast-iron pancakes you chipped your teeth on every morning. Check all that apply.

1. My camp had:
___ cabins
___ dirt bikes
___ trees
___ counselors
___ sky
___ food

2. For special occasions we got to:

___ make mud pies

___ eat mud pies

___ throw mud pies

___ make our
counselor's bed

___ sing "Kumbaya" *again*

___ help dredge the lake

3. To remember our great cabin, we bunkmates all exchanged:

___ phone numbers

___ addresses

___ hairbrushes

___ clothes

___ parents

___ family secrets

4. Next summer I'd really like to:

___ fold laundry

___ mow the lawn

___ come back to camp

Going Home

Good-bye, hill!
Good-bye, dale!
So long, ten-mile
dusty trail!
Good-bye, Moose!
Pixie, too!
You'll miss me.
Will I miss you?

What to Bring Home:

- ☐ flashlight
- ☐ socks
- ☐ shoes
- ☐ feet
- ☐ arts 'n' crafts projects
- ☐ new medications
- ☐ clothes
- ☐ stuff
- ☐ comics
- ☐ other stuff

What NOT to Bring Home:

- ☐ your bunkmate's cool sweatshirt
- ☐ your counselor's wallet
- ☐ your chigger collection
- ☐ your little rabid raccoon
- ☐ your cabinmate's underwear
- ☐ your used Band-Aid collection

Should You or Shouldn't You?

When camp counselors were surveyed, 100% checked *yes* in answer to the question: Should counselors get tips at the end of camp? So here are some tips we recommend:

Tip 1: Put all you've got on Jaunty Lady to win in the first race.

Tip 2: Never yell "Fire" in a crowded theater.

Tip 3: Coupons can save you up to 29% on your grocery bills.

Now go give Pixie or Moose that great camp handshake you learned and thank her or him for making your summer so . . . so . . . well, so long!

Katy Hall survived Camp Zoe in Missouri, Camp Miniwanka in Michigan, and Camp Lake Hubert in Minnesota. This book draws heavily on her real-life experiences in those summer camps. Ms. Hall now lives in New York City with her husband, an illustrator, and their fourteen-year-old daughter, who refuses to go to summer camp.

As a child, **Lisa Eisenberg** wisely avoided going away to summer camp. As a teenager, however, she worked as a counselor at Camp Brady in upstate New York. Her nightmarish memories of that summer were a great source of inspiration to her as she worked on this book. Today Ms. Eisenberg lives in Ithaca, New York, with her husband, a law professor, and her three children, ages 14, 10, and 6—all of whom *love* going to camp!

David Neuhaus never went to camp, perhaps because he wasn't allowed to bring his favorite toy, a model guillotine, with him. Consequently, he never experienced the joy of eating charbroiled marshmallows on a stick while sitting on a slimy log. Mr. Neuhaus lives in Fanwood, New Jersey, with his wife, a graphic designer, and their five-year-old daughter, who often camps out in the backyard.

Dear _____,

Whew! The bus finally made it to camp even though:

___ we all took turns driving.

___ the driver made a detour to Las Vegas.

___ the trip took two weeks.

___ we had to hitchhike the last ten miles.

___ the door is stuck and we're all still trapped inside.

___ I wasn't on it.

Help!

TO:

_____

_____

_____

The Camp Survival Handbook. Published by HarperCollins Publishers. Text copyright © 1995 by Katy Hall and Lisa Eisenberg. Illustration copyright © 1995 by David Neuhaus.

Dear _____,

Today we would have had our first swimming lesson except that:

___ the counselor passed out before she finished blowing up the pool.

___ no one thought to pack an ice pick.

___ we couldn't find the lake.

___ no way was I going to swim in a place called Piranha Lake.

___ the jellyfish wouldn't let us in.

Dry as ever,

TO:

_____

_____

_____

The Camp Survival Handbook. Published by HarperCollins Publishers. Text copyright © 1995 by Katy Hall and Lisa Eisenberg. Illustration copyright © 1995 by David Neuhaus.

MENU
TUNA SURPRISE
MEATBALL SURPRISE
LIVER SURPRISE
VEGGIE SURPRISE
FRUIT SURPRISE
DESERT SURPRISE
SURPRISE SURPRISE

GREETINGS FROM CAMP

Dear _____,

The food here is really unusual.
Tonight the cook served up:

___ instant mashed potatoes—poured
    straight from the box.

___ baked vermin-celli.

___ sauteed road kill.

___ possum surprise.

___ Odor-Eaters à la mode.

Send cookies!

TO:

_____

_____

_____

The Camp Survival Handbook. Published by HarperCollins
Publishers. Text copyright © 1995 by Katy Hall and Lisa
Eisenberg. Illustration copyright © 1995 by David Neuhaus.

Dear _____,

Camp is really great—especially
now that:

___ I'm out of the hospital.

___ my trunk showed up.

___ the swelling's gone down.

___ the killer bees flew south.

___ I've adopted a raccoon.

___ we've all been vaccinated.

Adiós,

TO:

_____

_____

_____

The Camp Survival Handbook. Published by HarperCollins
Publishers. Text copyright © 1995 by Katy Hall and Lisa
Eisenberg. Illustration copyright © 1995 by David Neuhaus.

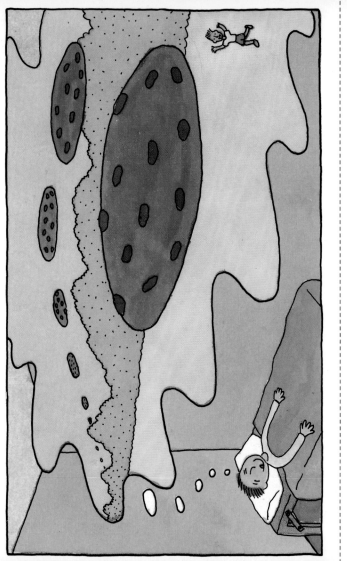

Dear _____ ,

Camp's okay, but it would be a lot better if you'd send:

___ cookies.

___ a whole box of cookies.

___ make it a big box.

___ filled to the brim.

___ two boxes would be okay.

___ those delicious chocolate chip cookies that only *you* can make.

___ double on the chips.

Your biggest cookie fan.

The Camp Survival Handbook. Published by HarperCollins Publishers. Text copyright © 1995 by Katy Hall and Lisa Eisenberg. Illustrations copyright © 1995 by David Neuhaus.

Dear _____ ,

Wow, how time has flown since I've been away at camp! Soon I'll be coming home. Gee, I hope you still recognize me with:

___ my bleached-orange spiked hair.

___ an extra 35 pounds from living on peanut butter all summer.

___ leeches covering 50% of my body.

___ my missing teeth.

___ that little surgical procedure the camp nurse tried on my nose.

I'm still your own.

The Camp Survival Handbook. Published by HarperCollins Publishers. Text copyright © 1995 by Katy Hall and Lisa Eisenberg. Illustrations copyright © 1995 by David Neuhaus.

KLUTZ
OF THE WEEK

SLOPPIEST
BUNK AWARD

THICKEST
TOOTH MOSS
IN CAMP!

**GREETINGS
FROM THE LAND
OF GIANT
MOSQUITOES**

NO BATH
THREE WEEKS AND COUNTING!

**?
WHEN ARE
YOU SENDING
MY TRUNK?**

#1
JUNK FOOD
COLLECTION

IN S'MORES-EATING
CONTEST
#1

**SEND
COOKIES
TODAY!**

**COUNSELOR'S
PET**